"Just know we all have stories worth your time. Just know we're just starting to understand our own worth." This is how Gayle Brandeis opens *Many Restless Concerns, Countess Bathory's Victims Speak in Chorus*. Countess Bathory of Hungary allegedly killed up to 650 girls and women between the years 1585 and 1609, in a variety of cruel, heartless ways. Brandeis brings these words to our attention--stab, strangle, pummel, hack, burn, drown, freeze, scald. "Your body remembers even when you no longer have a body, some tender part of you still flinches; some immaterial nerves still flare," she writes. "We want you to bear witness," voices the chorus. I urge you, the reader, to bear witness to these centuries of silent voices rising up clearly, often beautifully, more often tragically. Bear witness.
—Alma Luz Villanueva, author of *Song of The Golden Scorpion*

If all the women and girls who have been murdered, tortured, abused and disappeared were to raise their voices, they would create a song that would drown the world. In Gayle Brandeis' haunting and haunted novel-in-poems, *Many Restless Concerns*, she invokes such a chorus, the true story of hundreds of young women tortured to death by the Countess Bathory. Brandeis presents their gifts, their dreams, as well as the ways they died, and demonstrates that it is through collective action that they ultimately find justice. You will never un-hear their mournful, defiant and triumphal song.
—Terry Wolverton, author of *Embers*

Gayle Brandeis is a miracle. From the forgotten memories of murdered women, she's created a monument of hope, pain, and demands for the justice of recognition. This is a startling, glorious, gorgeous book. What a vision. Read this book and be transformed.
—Rene Denfeld, author of *The Child Finder*

Many Restless Concerns

The Victims of Countess Báthory Speak in Chorus

(A Testimony)

Gayle Brandeis

Black
Lawrence
Press

Black Lawrence Press

www.blacklawrence.com

Executive Editor: Diane Goettel
Cover Design: Peter Selgin
Cover Art: "Imagination" by Catrin Welz-Stein
Book Design: Amy Freels

Copyright © Gayle Brandeis 2020
ISBN: 978-1-62557-012-3

Published 2020 by Black Lawrence Press.
Printed in the United States.

"Many restless concerns came over me…"
—from *Last Will and Testament of Erzsébet Báthory*, September 3, 1610

"If they didn't take off their hair covering, if they did not start the fire, if they did not lay the apron straight…"
—from *Transcript of the Witness Interrogations Regarding the Cruel Deeds Which Erzsébet Báthory, Wife of Count Ferenc Nádasdy, is Accused*, 1611

Countess Erzsébet Báthory of Hungary was found guilty of killing as many as 650 girls and women between the years 1585 and 1609.

I

They say she bathed in our blood.

They say it brightened her complexion,
our iron and salt scouring her skin of impurities,
a bleach better than arsenic.

Or so you've heard.

                               (Or so everyone's heard.)

You've imagined her body a luminous petal in all that crimson—
hundreds of us bled for her beauty,
scores of us drained so she could glow.

If this were true, we wouldn't still hover here

                               (still haunt.)

If our blood had seeped into her skin,
we could have flowed directly into her heart,
tried to dampen its vicious thirst.
But our blood was ignored—
swabbed from marble floors,
left to sink into hard packed soil.
Our blood
(our dear and wasted blood)
our blood has trapped us here.

You want to know how we died.
> (That's all anyone wants to know,
> the harsh circumstance of our death.)

We will tell you
> (it's part of who we are, part of how we are)
but if that's all you want to know, don't waste our time. Leave now.
> Take your bloodlust elsewhere.

We want you to know how we lived. That we lived. That we were girls before we were game. That we were alive.

We were alive.

We were alive.

That we are still waiting for the release she thought she had given us.

We came from Pozsony and Predmier; we came from Nitra and Trencsén; we came from tiny villages you have never heard of, some of us sold into servitude by our parents, some for money, some for something as simple as a skirt (our body traded for a limp piece of cloth); some of us were found by scouts, flattered for our needlework, our millinery, our flair with sugar and flour; some of us were lured by the promise of a dowry, the promise of a merchant husband (all the boys and men of our villages gone to war); some of us were already employed at one Nádasdy estate or another before she arrived (Sárvár or Beckov or Keresztúr or Čachtice or the manor in Vienna). Some of us were ten, some seventeen. Some of us left home willingly; some had to be pulled from our mothers, our mothers who turned their heads so we wouldn't see their tears (or their relief). Some of us watched the land change from the carriage, the pastures and moors, the forests and fetid marshes; some of us kept our eyes closed as the carriage jostled us over the land. Some of us held our breath as we crossed the long bridge to the castle at Sárvár, mosquitos rising from the moat, or climbed the hill to the castle at Čachtice, the tilt pushing us back against our seats; some of us gasped as the giant doors opened. Some of us had never seen such opulence, the fine tapestries and golden fixtures and soaring paintings; some of us had never seen bowls full of pomegranates, platters piled with fancy cakes: some of us looked around at our new home and couldn't believe our luck.

II

We'd heard stories of torture. Stories about our great grandfathers, the 1514 revolt. Many were hanged or flayed, scarred in some permanent way; some were strapped to a wheel, bullwhipped, stabbed. Some were forced to eat their leader's roasted flesh after he was pushed upon a red hot iron throne, molten crown sizzling his scalp, scepter welding itself to his hand for daring to act like a king.

We cringed at the gore of these stories, thrilled (in secret, just a bit, just a bit) at the drama, cringing and thrilling as perhaps you are now. We never thought it could happen to us.

(You probably don't think it could happen to you, either, that sizzle of your own tortured skin.)

The lords passed laws to prevent more revolt, laws to chain our families to the land forever, braiding our bodies to wheat and grapes and sunflowers. From our first breath, we belonged to them, another product of their soil.

But tell that to a girl who felt life move through her limbs as she ran between rows of dill, scent clinging to her skirt, heart clanging into her ribs; tell that to a girl who knew her body was strong and whole and packed with sweet juice, a girl who knew being bound to this land was a gift even as it was a sentence.

You tell that girl her body is not her own.

Our bodies, we later learned, of course, were not our own. As much as we owned them then. As much we tried to hold on to them. But in the end, they were not hers, either. The land took them back. There is some comfort in that.

(Some)

Our great grandfathers were beaten
when they rose for their rights.
All we were doing was our jobs;
all we were accused of was our youth,
something we never knew we needed
to defend.

III

It's been thirty years since the killing began,
pools of blood forming beneath one girl after another
after another after another, fields freezing and thawing
and blooming and yielding and withering below us
again and again and again and again

thirty   years   like   one   long   terrible   day

We would be mothers
if we were still alive,
grandmothers
(some of us great.)
We would have lived
whole lives
upon the sweet
earth,
would have been
buried near
beloved bones.

IV

At first, it was only girls from Čachtice who gathered above the castle. We thrashed until we found each other, until we could settle into a sort of mist, soothe one another as the horror mounted. Then others found us, those killed at her other castles, those killed in carriages, those killed in villages along the way, the ones buried in shallow graves across the countryside, the ones pushed into rivers, the ones thrown into fire

(drawn like metal shavings to a magnet.)

Boys know this solidarity
when they go to war;
when do girls gather
in such numbers
in life?

Our edges have gone porous—we find ourselves knowing things
we hadn't before, pulling from one another's memory, from the
memory of the land below us—

still

some of us resist this merge
some of us remain firm enough
to peel ourselves away
some of us clot
into a temporary loneliness
so we can tell you
who we were

V

My father saw me watch him carve patterns in clay, saw me linger when he threw pine logs and grass in the furnace, when he covered the furnace with dirt to let the flame work its magic underground, turning his pots black and shiny as metal.

Black pottery is a craft passed from father to son, but my father had no son, and I had no mother, and he saw how I watched.

When he died, the clay saved me, its steady presence in my hands, its transformation in the fire, but I couldn't sell my pots and plates and cups, not once people learned who had made them, even though they were just as good as my father's had been. He would have told you that, himself. When recruiters for the Countess came to my town, how could I say no? How else could I survive? The scent of the furnace lingered on my clothes as I stepped into the carriage, lingered in my hair for days. I would pull my braid to my nose each night to help me sleep; when the smokiness left, I was lost.

***

I knew I'd be a horrible maid. I wouldn't know how to use any tool they might hand me—broom, needle, shovel, knife. My hands fumbled; I burned the bread, broke bowls I tried to wash. I could make up stories in my head, but what good is that in a castle? No one wants a maid telling tales (and I was no good at the telling—once the stories left my head, they turned to nothing but stammer.)

When bards called out

"Bone?"

to see if the crowd was listening, if the audience didn't yell

"Meat!"

in return, the storyteller knew he had lost them.

If I had found the breath to say "Bone," only silence would have answered. I was my own, my lone, audience, but I was happy in the small theater of my skull, the bone and the meat of me.

I didn't know how to do anything, not with my hands. My mother knew this, but she needed the money; my mother knew this, but she sent me away.

***

I had only embroidered samples before I was brought to Sárvár—patterns of diamonds and blocky flowers sewn on little squares of canvas—but I was confident in my work, my stitches smooth and tight. I knew I could transfer my skills to a skirt, a doublet, a bodice, a tapestry, whatever task was asked; I was eager for the chance to learn, develop my art. My fingertips were freckled with needle pokes, some deep enough to make me yelp.
I was prepared for more, thought it was the only risk I faced.

***

My father pounded bruises into my skin.
My father split my lip, blackened my eye, raised my skirts.
When I had the chance to work as a chambermaid,
I flew as if to the promised land.

***

After plum harvest, my whole village converged to make plum puree. We dragged giant copper cauldrons into the fields, poured in hundreds of plums, the fire underneath softening the fruit until it released its stone, until its scent deepened. We took turns stirring and stirring, straining out the pits, stirring without end, people stirring through the night, one week, sometimes two if the harvest was good, stirring and stirring one batch after another; if we stopped, the plums would burn, would ruin the whole pot, so we stirred and stirred, unending, passing the wooden paddle from one set of hands to another, stirring day and night and day and night, pouring the puree into large earthen pots, covering the pots with clean white paper, tumbling more plums into more pots, stirring more and more and more. Our arms ached, but it was my favorite time of year. I loved how the air smelled sweet and hot, smelled purple, loved how we all came together. Like now, but with muscle and scent. Girls and boys, men and women, laughter in all our mouths. The puree was so thick, we cut it into slices once it cooled, plunked a gleaming slab onto bread or ate it as it was, fingertips sticky and dark.

The scouts took me away one year just before the plums turned ripe.

VI

Some of us can't bear to share our own stories,
can't bear to remember what we've lost.
And could you bear hundreds of our stories?
Would you have the patience? The fortitude?
Would you grow immune to our pain,
turn numb after hearing from girl upon girl
upon tortured, murdered girl?

Let us spare you that numbness.

Just know we all have stories worth your time.
Just know we're starting to know our own worth.
Just know there is more to each of us
than you ever could have known.

VII

We were handed needles and knives and sugar and coal, handed shovels and thimbles and arms full of clothing, handed thread and stew pots and seeds for the garden, handed candles and brooms and serving forks and saffron and scissors and pigs' heads and wood for the fire; we were handed rags and fine linens and milling stones and chamber pots, handed hemp and bones and bread and irons.

Had we the nerve and unity we now share, we could have used those tools to rise up against her.

VIII

The Lady knew what it was like to leave home at a young age, sent to live with the Nádasdys at twelve so she could learn the ways of the estate before her wedding two years hence.

Does that give you sympathy for her? Have it if you must, have sympathy for poor, poor, Erzsébet Báthory (who had sympathy for none but herself).

She was an educated girl, more schooled than many princes. She could read Hungarian, Latin, German, maps; she could play the spinet, discuss issues of the day. She knew all the proper dances, all the ways to rouge one's cheek and pray to God. And she had fits, rages where she'd flail, scratch at her governess' eyes. The beast was alive in her from a tender age.

Perhaps it was alive in the whole Báthory family, perhaps that's why three wolf teeth slash across their coat of arms, three sharp and menacing points.

Countess Nádasdy taught her new things—how to stand for hours while girls like us hooked and tied her into her clothes, stained her lips with crushed beetles, dropped belladonna into her eyes to make them shine, applied wax to her hair so it would stay; how to hold court and send orders for cardamom to Vienna, how to manage hemp crops and write pleas to the king; how to plan a party; how take the waters in Piestany; how to keep her servants in their place.

The day of her wedding to Ferenc, Erzsébet and members of the bridal party, girls she barely knew, veiled their faces, paraded in front of the groom, each pretending to be her. Even Erzsébet pretended to be herself, pretended to be the bride she had been so carefully schooled to become. She knew she didn't belong at such a revel, her body tense inside her dress, blood spiked with a fierceness she didn't understand. The others mimed her as if she were a silly, mincing girl; they pranced before Ferenc, swung their hips, raised their arms as if ready to swoon.

She was ready to rip them apart.

She walked stiff in her frippery; she barely looked at her groom through her veil as she reached his chair, but he knew it was her; he lifted the veil, kissed her rigid, monstrous mouth.

She began to have children.
(Can you imagine?)

Anna, Orsika, Katalin, András, Pál.

Some say their wet nurse suckled
the Lady when she was a babe;
those poor children, fed on nothing
but curdle and dust.

Those poor children.

The Lady started small, a pinch here, a kick there. Nothing her mother in law hadn't taught her.

                            (Sometimes a bite.)

It grew worse after the Count returned from the battlefield, where he had danced with the bodies of his enemies, thrown and kicked their heads as sport, where he had learned tricks of torture from his foes, where he had acquired daggers studded with emeralds, curved sabers, gloves fitted with metal claws.

We learned to stay upright, to work even when wounds wept beneath our sleeves; we learned to keep our voices down, learned to not look her in the eye; we learned fear becomes another organ in the body, pulsing gall through every vein.

The Count died in battle—of a sudden illness, not a wound. (He wouldn't have liked that, his moment of glory stolen by his own body.) When news came to the Countess, something in her changed. She was calm at court, for visitors, ever the graceful widow, but alone, she seethed and stormed. She couldn't look at her children. She broke pots against the walls. She lashed her own back with nettles. She dropped to her knees and keened.

She rose and turned toward us.

IX

I was the first to die.

I don't know if she meant to kill; perhaps she was surprised her beatings could take life.

I can't help but wonder...had I been stronger, had I not succumbed, had I fought harder to stay inside my skin, would she have killed so many of us? My death stoked a hunger. She killed two more girls shortly after me, jammed all three of us in the same wooden box.

She told the preacher we had died of cholera, warned him not to open the coffin to avoid contagion. I was at the bottom of the box, the blood of us three girls mingling, staining one another's dresses, our bruises pressed against each other through our clothes, our hair tangled together. We were given a proper burial in the church cemetery; only the earliest of us to die were buried this way. The seminary students chanted hymns as they carried our shared coffin to the single hole in the ground, certain they were doing God's work.

***

I cleaned up her shit, her piss, her monthly blood. Doesn't matter how royal you are, you still shit and piss and bleed. Just like the horses whose stall I mucked back at home.

I carried her shit and piss and monthly blood; I tossed it out the window or took it to the garden. I knew she was animal like the rest of us, and she knew I knew this; she knew I could see through her fine clothes and airs. She knew I knew a crown is just a piece of metal, something you can stomp down flat, melt in the fire. She hated I could see this. She put me in the dirt where she thought I belonged.

***

I didn't work at the castle; I came to deliver *gomolya*—cheese from a ewe I had raised and milked, milk I had strained, warmed with the lining of a calf's fourth stomach until curds separated from whey, curds I poured into cloth, hung from the eaves for five days, changing the cloth daily as the whey dripped sour puddles; cheese I let ripen for three weeks in the sun; cheese I stored on a wooden board to make it taste of the forest; *gomolya* I was so proud to bring to the castle, hoping to secure my family's fate.

***

I was polishing candlesticks when she asked me to polish the statue. I had been afraid of that statue even before I learned what it held, afraid of the blonde hair
(real hair, our hair)
that glistened from the head and between the legs of its dark iron body.

The Countess watched as I swept my cloth over the thing's rough curves, her eyes etching chills into my skin. When I rubbed the left breast, it triggered clockworks, spiking my flesh so instantly, it almost didn't hurt. It almost felt like a shocking stab of truth, the kind you aren't ready to accept.

X

You hear words like *burn* and *drown* and *freeze* and *scald* and they're just words to you. You hear *stab* and *strangle* and *pummel* and *hack* and they're just words, too. A few letters, easy to say. Easy to move past. *Burn. Drown. Freeze. Scald.* Compact little sounds. Some may make you flinch. Send a momentary shiver down your body, raise a bit of gooseflesh. But then your nerves settle; your body seals itself again.

When your body knows these words, knows them in every fiber, the words change. They become the smell of your own scorched skin, the taste of your own blood, the sight of your own fingers on the floor, separate as dropped slices of apple. These words have become something more than words. They have become weapons, ready to get under the surface of you, pry you back open.

Your body remembers even when you no longer have a body

(some tender part of you still flinches)
(some immaterial nerves still flare)

XI

We found little moments of comfort. Moments when we could slip a scrap of bread beneath a cube of bacon roasting and catch its drippings; moments when we could pass poultices of comfrey or yarrow or burdock between us, take a breath or two of sweet relief. Moments when we could look into each other's eyes, even for a flash. And there were days, blessed days on end, when she was off at another estate, or at court, or the spa, days when her worst lackeys were not around to carry out her orders, and we could shape the marzipan however we wanted or toast corn kernels to share as a treat, or take a moment to rest in our washing and look out the window, or linger in the herb garden, breathing in the marjoram and rosemary and tarragon; times when we didn't need to worry if our aprons were straight, our hair perfectly in place; times when we could rub our hands if they cramped during our sewing; times when we could talk to one another, sometimes even laugh; times when we could go out to the orchard and eat every pear we wanted.

XII

You wonder about her children. What she said to explain the screams, the blood on her clothes, the monks hurling pots against her walls to protest cries inside.

We don't know. Perhaps the governess whispered fairy tales at night. We do know as the children grew, they came to learn the truth.

The night before Katalin, the youngest daughter, married, the Lady brought two of us into her chamber, showed her daughter how to burn us. (An initiation. A married woman must know how to discipline her staff.)

Kati took to it right away. The two of us died during the wedding party. Guests saw our bodies being carried away, but the Lady (as always) had her excuses; the guests nodded and toasted the newly-weds; the guests nodded and continued to dance.

XIII

It almost seemed like a joke. She made me get in a giant pot. (Funny, yes?) Me, who spent so much time making pots, although she didn't know this. I wasn't brought here as a potter, the smoke long gone from my hair. The pot was simply what was closest, what compelled her. She made me get in. It wasn't a well-made pot, certainly not the shiny black I formed with my own hands. This was a tall, big-bellied pot, crudely shaped. It came to my hips. I'd seen kitchen girls make pickles in jars of a similar shape, only smaller. They would place a slice of bread at the top of the jar, a slice of dark bread. (I don't know why; perhaps to keep out flies.) They removed the bread when it was time to rinse the pickles before their second round of ferment; it was just a sour sponge by then, a soggy mess. I saw a kitchen girl eat it, looking around to make sure no one was watching; it fell apart in her hands, dripped brine on her skirt. But pickles were not in this pot, I was. (Funny, yes? A girl's head sticking out from a giant pickle jar?) Someone had slapped this pot together—the edges irregular, a finger print here and there. When I climbed in, the roughness of the lip scraped a strip of skin from my leg. It was tricky to get the other leg in; the pot wobbled as I entered it. I wondered if it would fall, but it quickly righted itself. She bade me crouch down so my body filled the curve of the pot. I could smell the inside of it, the cool earth of it, and it made my hands long for clay, all its damp comforts. Then she poured in the boiling water—just like with pickles, yes? (Still funny?) At least with pickles, you let the water cool after you boil it; you give the cucumbers that one small mercy; you let the water cool before you pour it in the jar.

XIV

She wanted only virgins, girls who hadn't known the pleasures of love. But how could she tell who among us had been touched?

Some of us had sweethearts before we came here. Some brought us to bliss with a mere kiss behind the ear. Some had rough fingers; some of us liked that. Some slipped their hands beneath our shirts, found the tips of our breasts, made us shiver and squirm. Some knew how to touch us between the legs and turn us to liquid fire. Some shoved themselves into us before we knew what was happening. Some cleaned the blood from our thighs later. Some cleaned only themselves, never looked our way again.

Some of us were the virgins she wanted, sealed like an apricot. No one had touched us there before she did—a few, not even ourselves, other than to clean, and then only quickly (as if to avoid a burn).

Some of us had found love with other girls in our villages. A few of us even found love in the castle—rare moments of rapture in dark corners.

Some of us had been torn by soldiers—Turk, Hussar, Hajduk, some soldiers from our own villages, emboldened by their uniforms. Uniforms that changed the boys we knew

(boys who changed what we knew of ourselves).

She wanted only virgins at first, but in the end, she just wanted bodies (bodies that hadn't been touched, bodies that had—no matter, long as hers was the last our bodies knew).

She knew I wasn't a virgin, knew I was wed, a mother, but I was her pet. She dressed me like a young girl, invited me to serve at her fanciest parties, trusted me with her costliest jewels. I was her pet until I told her my breasts were hard with milk, said I had to go home to my babe. She grabbed a log from the wood pile, thrust it in my arms.

"This is your babe," she said. "Suckle."

I laughed, sure this was a joke, but she yanked the top of my blouse down, shoved the wood against my breast, rasping my nipple. Milk spilled, freeing the scent of hazel from the bark.

"Your Grace," I started.

"Don't let it cry," she said through gritted teeth,
and rammed the wood closer to my heart.

XV

She wanted us to disappear into the pain, wanted to engulf us with it, wanted it to obliterate everything we ever had been, everything we ever could be. But strange thing about pain—it can make the world disappear, but it can also open a magnificence inside your body, a terrible magnificence that makes you feel infinite, as if you're blasting out in all directions, hurtling toward the stars.

(And maybe you are.)

XVI

I came from Tokaj, like the wine. People say gold lives in the ground there, pushes its way up into the grapes, so when you drink our wine, you drink drops of pure gold. My grandparents told me Paracelsus, the Swiss alchemist, came to Tokaj in 1524 to conduct experiments. He wrote, "In the grapes of Hegyalja, the vegetable and mineral substances are mingled. The light of the sun shines like a golden thread through the vine and its roots into the rock." He thought the gold came from the sun, that it trickled its way down through the grapes into the soil, the opposite of what people in Tokaj believed.

The grapes did have a vein of it through them, a hard little vein of gold when the grapes were slightly overripe, which is what the wine called for, the grapes ready to fold into themselves, gold stiffening inside. I roamed the vineyards with my mother as she worked, helping her pick, popping a few grapes in my mouth as we traversed the rows, gold catching, sticky, between my teeth. Sweetness flooded through me and I imagined the gold had lodged itself somewhere inside my body, that it shined in the dark places between my bones and made me a special girl.

I was brought to the castle to work the vineyards. The grapes at Čachtice are nothing like Tokaj grapes. No gold, the fruit tart and shivery on the tongue. The gold in me faded, too. I learned to not eat the grapes as I worked—they leached all the water from my mouth— but she still thought I was stealing from her vines, still shoved bunches of fruit down my throat.

Paracelsus believed there is a *principia* in all things:
"A nature," he wrote, "a force,
a virtue, and a medicine,
once, indeed, shut up within things,
but now free from any domicile
and from all outward incorporation...
It is a spirit like the spirit of life,
but with this difference,
that the life-spirit of a thing is permanent,
but that of man is mortal."

He was backwards in this, too.

He couldn't have envisioned us all here together,
life-spirits distilled from our mortal girl bodies
(herbs condensed to their most pungent essential oil.)

Nettle grows in abundance near every single one of her castles
(by design or chance, we do not know.)
*

Our mothers made us nettle tea for colds, for cramps, for sour bellies,
the drink sharp and dank and soothing.
*

The Lady made whips of nettle, lashed strings of prickle across our
backs, raised bubbles of itch and burn.
*

Our mothers showed us how to pick the tender leaves at the top of the
nettle plant, boil them into soup. If the nettles bored into our hands,
our mothers would rub our palms with onions or mud, sometimes
their own spit.
*

She wrapped herself in nettles, asked us to touch the thorns, our fin-
gers grazing close to her skin; she asked us to push them in deeper. She
closed her eyes—she seemed to relish the sting—but then she opened
them again; she wanted to see our own eyes as the plant jabbed into
our fingers.
*

Our mothers drank nettle tea to help us grow in their bellies; they
drank nettle tea to make milk when we were new. When we started to
walk, they chewed nettle leaves to a soft mash, pressed them against
any scrape or bruise.
*

She scattered nettles on the stone floor, made us roll in them after she
had broken us open, barbs searing each wound.
*

Our mothers would say "csalánba nem üt a mennykő"—no lightning
strikes the nettle; bad things elude bad people. They said it sometimes
with a wistful sigh, sometimes a jolt of anger.

(We hoped they didn't really mean it.
We hoped in this they weren't right.)

XVII

There are three worlds, we were taught—
the upper world, where angels bathe in lakes of milk,
the lower world, where dragons dwell in darkness,
the human world afloat between.

If this is true, we are stuck halfway up,
                          not quite human,
                              not quite angel,
            keen to taste the milk of paradise
on what used to be our tongues.

XVIII

The Lady demanded we leave our quarters to make room for her daughter Anna's staff in advance of their visit. Her henchwoman Dorka stripped five of us down, herded us to the room where coal was stored, where coal spilled from its bins, the dirt floor heaped with it, the air choked with its mineral scent. Maybe we could have fought back—five of us to one—but we'd seen what Dorka could do.

The coal was hard, bumpy beneath our bare feet. Wherever we tried to rest, stones burrowed into our skin. If we tried to walk, coal wobbled us. We reached out to grab onto one another, to give each other help, but sometimes we pulled each other down.

"What do we do?" one of us asked.
"We're dead," one of us said; the rest of us shivered.
"She'll come for us," one of us who hadn't been in the castle long said. "She'll need us and come for us."

But she didn't.
She didn't come and she didn't come and she didn't come.
She didn't come and our mouths grew dry.
She didn't come and our stomachs whined, then panged, then went numb.
She didn't come and the air grew thicker, our piss and sweat and shit adding to, intensifying, the scent of coal.
She didn't come and we picked our way through the dark and huddled together as the room grew colder.
She didn't come and we crawled away from the group to relieve our bodies,

or try to move toward fresher air, coal rolling below, biting into, our
    knees.
She didn't come and we always came back to each other's skin,
the only softness in the room.
She didn't come until we couldn't move at all.

When Dorka finally opened the door, the light made us flinch.

"The Lady is traveling to the spa with her daughter," barked Dorka.
"She needs maidservants," but we could no longer lift our heads.

The Countess was furious—it was fine to cut us, to burn us, but we
still had to be able to work. She spooned broth into our mouths until
we could sit. Then she beat us until we died.

Our five bodies were pushed under a bed. There were too many of us to carry away, try to bury, without someone noticing. The washer-woman had a tender heart; she left food next to the bed every day, as if we could still chew and swallow, as if we could still taste the roast pork, the salad of pressed cabbage, the bread fried crisp in lard. Maybe she felt guilty she couldn't feed us the week we were held in the coal room. Dorka had bade thunder slay anyone who dared bring us nourishment.

(The food rotted right along with us.)

XIV

She cinched my hands numb with rein straps, wrapped my hair around the iron bars across the window, let me dangle from it, hairs pinging from my head with a *pop pop pop* like water dropped in hot oil, every inch of scalp burning. I watched my hands turn blue and thought of the blue trout she loved, how I would loop a string between its lower jaw and tail, curving the fish into an arc, how I would stud an onion with cloves, add it to the simmer of white wine and peppercorns and herbs, how I would gently rinse the trout before I lowered it slowly into the broth; if I damaged the skin, it wouldn't turn blue, the way she loved it, the blue trout I doused with boiling vinegar once I removed it from the kettle, then placed on the platter as if it were leaping from the boiled potatoes, fixed in a moment of grace.

We looked down, watched her lackeys pour water over girls' naked bodies, ruddy in the snow.

We yelled "No! Stop!" but our voices were nothing in the cold air, not even puffs of steam.

We couldn't stop them, couldn't stop her, but we could be there for the girls as the ice closed around their faces, tightened around their arms; we could be there as their spirits cracked their way through the ice and darted about, frightened and confused, zigging and zagging like lightning bugs.

"We're here," we whispered until they could hear us. "We're like you. We are you."

Their spirits turned from the snow, saw us floating overhead. They hesitated at first, wanted to stay tied to the frozen evidence of their lives, but eventually they loosened their hold upon their flesh; eventually they tendrilled up to join us.

Are we making this too pretty?
We don't want to make this too pretty.
We don't want to turn our deaths into spectacle.
We don't want to excite you with our pain.
We know people will remember her, not us.
We want you to bear witness.
We want this to be an epitaph
over all our unmarked graves.

XX

I washed great quantities of blood in the laundry, her clothes often stained with it. I'd watch blood drift into the water around my hands, tinge it the palest pink. The rest, I'd have to scrub. Sometimes it didn't come out all the way. Sometimes she used those clothes as bribes to get more girls to the castle. Peasant mothers didn't mind a stain or two on a fine dress. It could easily have been beet soup, they reckoned, meat juice, wine.

I scrubbed and scrubbed, trying to remove the stains. I scrubbed and scrubbed, taking some of our blood under my fingernails, taking some of our pain into my arms until I could barely move from the ache of it, but kept going. I scrubbed and scrubbed and scrubbed and scrubbed, as if I could erase what she'd done.

XXI

Rumors spread.

Mothers hid their daughters when the Lady or her servants came scouting. Some mothers were dragged away, themselves, tied up until they relented, relinquished their young.

The scouts had to trek farther and farther, looking for desperate girls, hopeful girls, girls who had yet to hear of the Lady's wrath.

In Vienna, I pinned a yellow ring to my clothes when I went out in public, a yellow ring the Emperor designed to mark me Jew. Jews found without the ring had to forfeit our clothes, forfeit whatever we carried, sometimes (often) more. We could only live in the Jewish quarter, could only hold certain jobs. I was thrilled when I was invited to the castle, thrilled when I was told I could remove the yellow pin as I stepped into the carriage. I didn't want to remove my faith, only my restriction, wanted to live a bigger life than the one Ferdinand had prescribed for me.

I hoped I could light Sabbath candles at the castle, hoped the Lady was a kind and tolerant soul.

XXII

The Countess may have read many languages, but she could not speak all of ours—not Slovak nor Croatian nor Romany. She wanted her staff to speak Hungarian, but over time, she couldn't afford to be as particular. If we couldn't understand her, she found other ways to make herself known. The sounds she pried from our bodies required no interpretation.

(Some of us grew up
saying "anya", some "mutter"
but here, we understand
each other perfectly;
here, languages merge
into single polyphonic
mother tongue.)

XXIII

burn...............
......*drown*............
.......................*freeze*..............
.........*scald*..............
....*stab*..........................
.....................*strangle*.....................
....*pummel*..........
...................*hack*....................
......*burn*...
.............................*stab*...........................
............*drown*.....................................
................................*strangle*..................
....*freeze*....................
...*pummel*...
...........................*scald*........................
....*hack*....................
.......do you feel the words now?...................................
.............do you shrug them away? slough them off?..........
...what if we scream *BURN! DROWN! FREEZE! SCALD!*....
.........can you feel them now?........................
STAB!STRANGLE!PUMMEL!HACK!..................................
...............what will make you understand?...............
..................we are *GONE!*................
....................we are *GONEGONEGONEGONEGONEGONEGONE!*

XXIV

You want to know if the worst rumors are true.
You want to know if she lit candles, pulled irons from ovens,
if she pinned us down and rent our clothes
and burned our innermost, most intimate place.
It's what some people have whispered about, wondered about, the
most.

(We can hear it. We can hear you wondering.)

Try to imagine.
Just try to imagine how that felt.

Imagine the sun entering your body.
Not a gentle warm sun.
Not a sun that drenches you with heat and sweat.
Imagine the whole brutal inferno yanked from the sky
and shoved into your very center, annihilating you
from the inside out.

Even that doesn't come close.

(Why did we even try?)

Bone?
Bone?

Are you still there?

Bone?

We know this is rough. But you can take it.
It's only words, yes?

Words can be hard to bear, we know.
Even if you haven't lived them,
some words can be hard to bear.

But you can do it.

There is more you can do,
more you can take,
than you can imagine now.

Your body can carry more
than you'll ever know.

XXV

Have you heard the story of Szelemen?
He was stolen by Turks, our grandmothers
told us, forced to work for a rich man
           (not unlike us)
sent to work in the apple orchard.
Do not eat the apples, he was warned,

and he tried not to.
           (Was his master as cruel as our Lady?
           Did he fear his master's wrath?)
But one day, his mouth was parched,

his whole body sapped,
and he knew a bit of sweetness
would enliven him, his work.
           (What harm could one little apple do?)
But when he bit into the fruit,
he found no sugar, no crunch, no juice;
raw human flesh filled his mouth,
the apple an enchanted girl.

Would we rather
she had turned us
into apples?

Perhaps.

Trapped
but solid,
able to feel
rain and wind
on our skin,
able to feel ourselves
soften with age,
a quick melt
to earth
when we fell.

XXVI

Perhaps you're ready for this now.

Has anyone whispered about this, too?
They way she carved chunks from some of our bodies,
forced a kitchen girl to cook the pieces with mushrooms and wine?
The way she sometimes fed it to guests unsuspecting as Szelemen,
mixed into sausage or stew? The way she sometimes made us
swallow it, ourselves?

(Did she take inspiration from 1514,
our great grandfathers forced to eat their leader?
Did she take inspiration from fables,
all that enchanted fruit?)

It's hard to bring yourself to eat your own body.
You can imagine this, can't you? How hard it would be?
It's only a bit easier if you're starving.

(Some of us were.)

Does this make you cringe?
Make you dizzy, make you ill?
We would apologize,

but this is true.
(It's not a fable—
we had to live it.)

It's only words for you;
if you don't take them in,
this (or something like it)
could happen to more women,
more girls. Over and over
and over and over
if we don't speak
of these things.

Bone?
Bone?
Bone?
Bone?

Will you answer us with "Meat"?
With all the meat of you?

XXVII

Things we miss:

Our heartbeat in our wrists, our throats, our breasts. A deep breath that fills our whole body. Bare feet against wet stone. Bare feet against mud. The crunch of boots against snow. The scent of bread baking. Butter melting on bread. Warm, dry clothes after being out in the cold. Washing our face after a long day of work. Drinking water after a long walk. The breath of flowers in a garden. The electric press of our arm next to someone else's. A perfectly cooked egg. Feeling returning to our fingers by the fire. Soup, using hollowed bread crust as a spoon. The scent of raspberries boiling for juice. Polenta with roasted bacon. Our mother's voice.

(This is too hard.
We need to stop.)

XXVIII

You keep wondering about pain.
You can't get past it, the pain she rained down upon us.

The pain was _____

                              The pain was _____

            The pain was_____

The pain was _____

                              The pain was _____

We could keep trying, but the words don't exist.
(Even if you think you understand, you don't.)

XXIX

The elite didn't grasp
what was happening
in the castle.

(Why should they care
when peasant girls
go missing?)

They only noticed
when their own girls
disappeared.

My mother told me I sang in the womb. When I was born, I didn't cry, she said—I let out a perfect, pure note that filled the house with light.

It was a gift; I didn't own my voice, couldn't be vain about its beauty. It flowed through me, divine river. It poured from my mouth like gold. I was clumsy when not singing, awkward, barely could stammer a sentence, but when I sang, I went incandescent.

I was doing what God had asked of me.

People closed their eyes in rapture when my voice rang through the church, ears and hearts tuned to God's grace.

News of my gift reached the Countess. She invited me to her home in Vienna for a private concert, a command performance in her parlor. My mother brought me to the door, but the Countess let only me inside; she sent my mother home, said a messenger would come when we were through. My mother saw my hesitation and kissed my forehead, whispered this could lead to bigger appearances, more money. I let the Countess usher me inside the broad hall.

Some servant girls eyed me. I smiled, hoping my voice would be a balm for their day of hard work, but they looked down, looked away.

The Countess walked briskly toward a room filled with red settees. I raced to keep up, trying not to lose my breath before my performance.

She closed the heavy wooden door behind us.

She sat down and said, "Sing."

She said it the way she would ask someone to sweep her floor or fasten her corset. A demand, eyes cold. And as I stood before her, I felt my gift leave me. My mouth turned dry; my throat froze.

"Sing!" she said again. This time, a threat.
I opened my lips, but no sound came out.
I opened my lips, but God had abandoned me.

The Countess opened the Gynaeceum, a finishing school for elite young ladies. Our parents jumped at the chance to send us—they wanted us to learn etiquette before they sent us off to royal court.

In ancient Greece, a gynaeceum was a place for women to retreat, to have a private life, a place where a lady and her servants could relax and talk together, feel safe.

Gyaneceum: "of or belonging to women."

Our Gyaneceum was different. It didn't belong to us; we belonged to her as soon as we walked through her door. She didn't even pretend to teach us.

The entire student body was dead within weeks.

XXX

She asked the forest witch to make her invisible. The forest witch had no spell to render her transparent, but gave her a special recipe, a cake that would make her untouchable.

The Lady enlisted me, her best baker, to prepare it.

The Lady stripped off her clothes, climbed into my baking trough, the large metal bin where I'd mix great quantities of dough (though not as big as the troughs used in my village during feast time, troughs deep as castle moats, troughs where we would make bread tall as a man, cooked on glowing embers in the earth, blanketed with ash). It was strange to see her naked in my kitchen, pale as raw bread dough. She looked so soft, so easy to break. (And how I wanted to. How I wanted to grab one of my knives and end her, end her right there by the potatoes and thyme.) When she asked me to pour water over her, I was tempted to scald her, to freeze her, as I had seen her do to some of us, but she insisted upon a certain temperature and Dorka would have wrestled the pot from me if she knew it was too hot, would have thrown it against my own skin.

(Please forgive my lack of nerve.)

The Lady bathed in the trough long enough for her filth to taint the water, taint the cakes I would make from it. The cakes—which I braided like pretzels as the forest witch had instructed—turned a revolting shade of gray, as if her evil had infected each crumb, although the gray was likely from the powder she commanded I add, the foul smelling powder the forest witch claimed had protective powers. The ugliest cakes I've ever made, but she insisted upon serving them to the Palatine and the Judge—one cake for each man—when they came to visit after the parents of the Gyaneceum girls amongst us demanded it. (Parents of the peasant girls amongst us had also demanded action, but of course the Palatine hadn't listened.)

Before the men arrived, the Lady set a communion wafer in the center of each cake—she called it a mirror, said she could see the faces of her enemies within it, clear as day. She stood over the cakes and chanted for an hour, chanted the spell the witch had taught her to make her invisible to the reach of law.

The Palatine and the Judge looked askance at the cakes, as they well should have, and flinched when they each took a taste; sugar could only hide so much of the powder's bite. They became ill after just one small forkful each, quickly retired to their quarters.

Had I known (I should have known) her intention was to poison, I would have found a way to change the recipe, make it safe for the men who could be our only hope. I would have poured the powder next to the trough, substituted clean water. I didn't do any of this, but she blamed me, killed me, anyway, for their refusal to eat more cake.

She waited until they left so as not to raise suspicion, but their suspicions were already well-raised. As their carriage clattered away, the wind whispered

stop her, stop her

but it wasn't the wind at all.

XXXI

The men looked around the carriage,
looked at each other.

They had heard us.
Both of them had heard us.

After all these years of floating,
watching, trying to shout,
they had heard us.

Maybe we'd reached a number
that had tipped the scales,
the weight of all
us weightless girls
finally given voice.

XXXII

A girl escaped the castle, a knife plunged deep in her foot. We felt her heart race from all the way up here in the sky, felt it as if we still had hearts in our chests, as if we still had chests to hold those hearts. Some of us left our cluster to follow her, try to protect her.

(We could do this now.
We'd grown some
invisible muscle.)

We did what we could to surround her as she hobbled down the hill to town, foot red with blood, looking over her shoulder every few steps; the bottoms of her feet red now, too, from the rocks and twigs beneath them; she could barely stand, but we kept her going; we led her to a barber who removed the knife, sewed the wound, sent word to the Palatine; we led her in such a way she could think something in her was leading herself, some part that knew the path in this unfamiliar town, even in her state of shock. We cheered for her in such a way she thought it was coming from inside her, her blood rushing the roar of a crowd in her ears.

XXXIII

The Countess stood beneath the stars with the forest witch, looked
to the dark sky.
She wavered, as if in trance. She closed her eyes and chanted:

Help me, O Clouds!
O Clouds, stay by me!
Don't let any harm come
to Erzsébet Báthory,
let her remain healthy and invincible!

She didn't know what she was wishing for.

She didn't see the cloud of girls above her,
gathering like a sea of feathers.
gathering like a storm,
a constellation of murdered girls
phosphorescent in our rage.

XXXIV

And then the day came.
The swarm of carriages, of men.

Some of us swooped down, helped lead the men to the rooms where we were tortured, nudging their shoulders, whispering in their ears. We led them to our bodies shoved into grain bins, our bodies buried in shallow garden graves; we led them to our bodies stacked in tunnels, piled in wooden crates. We held their hearts so they could handle the sight, calmed their bellies so they could handle the scent; we bolstered their arms so they could lift our bodies, carry us toward rest.

The Lady tried to charm, to blame, but they bound her hands, dragged her to the cellar where many of our bodies had been found.

A live girl was found there, too.

A girl barely alive, a girl who had started to leave her body, who had begun to float toward us, but was sucked back inside her skin. The men found her shackled to a table. One hand was mangled, big hunks gouged from her shoulders, her backside. The men weren't sure she was breathing when they first entered the room, but when they broke the restraints, she released a small sigh, cracked one eye open. We slipped between her ribs, fortified her heart, her blood, willed air into her lungs. We chanted deep inside her, like a pulse:

Live. Live. Live. Live.

XXXV

They didn't name many of us during the trial.

A few of us were identified—the Gyaneceum students; the "Sittkey girl", killed for stealing a pear—but most of us were called nothing more than "servant girl", "seamstress", "chambermaid", "girl."

Many of us don't remember our own names now.
(They are the among the first things to fade.)

It's fine you don't know our names now.
You know our testimony.
You know enough to yell "Meat!"
when we call out "Bone?"

if you are listening.

(Are you still listening?)

You know enough to lay some flesh upon our forgotten skeletons,
to feel the weight of our deaths inside your own body.

You know enough to remember how alive you are
(how lucky).

XXXVI

"You, Erzsébet, are like a wild animal," the Palatine declared at the end of the trial.

"You are in the last months of your life," he said. "You do not deserve to breathe the air on earth or see the light of the Lord."

He said, "You shall disappear from the world and shall never reappear in it again."

He said, "As the shadows envelop you, may you find time to repent your bestial life."

He said, "I hereby condemn you, Lady of Čachtice, to lifelong imprisonment in your own castle."

She was locked in a room, a slot carved into the door to deliver meals. We squeezed into the space with her, pressed against the ceiling, but our strength had dissipated, drained by the help we had given. We tried to speak, but our voices had left us, our share of earthly volume spent.

She had asked to be imprisoned in her wedding gown, and with time, it began to chafe. She couldn't remove it; she had never undressed herself—we always had to help her undo the ties and stays, pull the corsets from her body. It gave us some satisfaction to watch her twist and yank and snarl, trapped in that fine cloth.

(If we could, we would have ripped it all to shreds.)

She was there longer than the Palatine predicted—
over three years we spent
plastered to that ceiling,
a blink, an eon, a blur, a bore.
Our vision dimmed
(everything in us dimmed)
as her dress disintegrated,
as she peeled it like bandages
from her skin.

XXXVII

More of us found our way to the castle.
Our cloud began to spread across the ceiling,
began to regain some strength.
Our vision sharpened again, focused.
Now we could see her untouched meals.
Now we could see her crouch in the corner,
hair greasy, matted, cheeks sunken.
Now we were glad we could no longer smell.

We watched her bite her nails
until her fingers bled,
skin slack on her bones,
naked as she'd forced us to be.

A pitiful animal.

(The animal that had always lived inside her,
the skinned hare trembling inside the beast.)

And then a surge.

We all felt it; something like anger
(something like mercy)
burned through the mass of us,
melting whatever sap
had held us fast.

We dropped down,
closed in
all around her;
we crowded out
what was left
of the air.

XXXVIII

When her spirit left her body, it looked at us a moment,
                                        then turned away.

(Out of shame or disgust or something else, we'll never know.)

She disappeared right after, faded into nothing.

                        (Even in death, she was granted a freedom
                                        we were not.)

We threw ourselves around the room,

                                         a frenzy

                                                       desperate

for escape.

                            We flailed

                                                              and

          shrieked

                              and

thrashed

                    and

                                                yowled

and

          flailed

                            and

                                        shrieked

                and

thrashed

                            and

                yowled

until you opened the door

                  and peered inside

              and something in us

                      stilled, held breath

        that wasn't breath;

you opened the door
and peered inside
and we knew why
we were still here.

It was so we could speak to you.

XXXIX

We feel ourselves grow lighter now

(a fade)

(*a shimmer*)

(maybe our blood
hasn't kept us here;
maybe our story, unheard,
had glued us to this world)

(maybe the spill of blood
demands the spill of story)

(maybe story is the blood of ghosts)

XXXX

We start to seep through

      the walls of the castle,

              a chain of us;

                  we start to drift over the countryside

                      a span of thinning cloud

We look down,
see the girl whose heart we enlivened.

The judge had granted her a farm near the castle,
her own farm and fifteen pounds of wheat.
We see her outside, the wheat high as her breast.

She pauses in the field.

We can almost smell the rich soil,
almost feel the plants tickle our palms.

She looks up

She lifts a hand
as if in greeting
      (or farewell)

and then all

we can see

is sun

Acknowledgments

I am grateful to my daughter Hannah for her interest in notorious women of history, which led me to discover Countess Báthory, and the hundreds of girls and women she silenced.

I am grateful to all my family and friends for your love and understanding as I dove into this grisly subject matter (with a special nod to dear friend and long time first reader Laraine Herring, who believed in and supported this project from its inception in 2009).

I am grateful to Kimberly L. Craft for her extensive research about Countess Báthory, and for her permission to include her translations in this book (the epigraph, the cloud chant, and the Palatine's declaration). Clark's books *Infamous Lady: The True Story of Countess Erzsébet Báthory* and *The Private Letters of Countess Erzsébet Báthory* were especially helpful.

I am grateful for other books that provided invaluable research along the way: *The Sword and the Crucible: Count Boldizsar Batthyany and Natural Philosophy in Sixteenth-century Hungary* by Dóra Bobory, *Culinaria Hungary: A Celebration of Food and Tradition* by Anikó Gergely, *The Bloody Countess* by Valentine Penrose, *Beloved Children: History of Childhood in Hungary in the Early Modern Age* by Katalin Peter, and *Countess Dracula* by Tony Thorne. I took liberties with this research, of course—this is a work deeply informed by history, but is very much a work of imagination.

I am grateful to Diane Goettel and the rest of Black Lawrence Press for giving this project such a good home.

I dedicate this book to disappeared and murdered women throughout history, across the globe, including the thousands of missing and murdered indigenous US and Canadian women whose cases have not been given enough attention.

> May your names be remembered.
> May your stories be told.
> May we make the world a safer place for all girls and
> women to come.

In addition to *Many Restless Concerns,* Gayle Brandeis is the author, most recently, of the memoir *The Art of Misdiagnosis* (Beacon Press), and the poetry collection *The Selfless Bliss of the Body* (Finishing Line Press). Earlier books include *Fruitflesh: Seeds of Inspiration for Women Who Write* (HarperOne) and the novels *The Book of Dead Birds* (HarperCollins), which won the Bellwether Prize for Fiction of Social Engagement judged by Barbara Kingsolver, Toni Morrison, and Maxine Hong Kingston, *Self Storage* (Ballantine), *Delta Girls* (Ballantine), and *My Life with the Lincolns* (Henry Holt BYR), which was chosen as a state-wide read in Wisconsin. Her poetry, essays, and short fiction have been widely published in places such as *The New York Times, The Washington Post, O (The Oprah Magazine), The Rumpus, Salon, Longreads,* and more, and have received numerous honors, including a Barbara Mandigo Kelly Peace Poetry Award, Notable Essays in *Best American Essays 2016* and *2019,* the QPB/*Story Magazine* Short Story Award and the 2018 Multi Genre Maverick Writer Award. She teaches at Sierra Nevada College and Antioch University Los Angeles.